DIESTERWEG
FIRST
READERS

Amy Frances Koerner

Ruby's story

westermann

© 2015 Westermann Bildungsmedien Verlag GmbH,
Georg-Westermann-Allee 66, 38104 Braunschweig
www.westermann.de

Druck A^5 / Jahr 2023
Alle Drucke der Serie A sind im Unterricht parallel verwendbar.

Redaktion: Doris Bos, Jutta Eckardt-Scheurig, Amy Koerner
Illustrationen: Ulf Marckwort, Kassel
Umschlagkonzeption: blum design und kommunikation, Hamburg
Druck und Bindung: Westermann Druck Zwickau GmbH,
Crimmitschauer Straße 43, 08058 Zwickau

ISBN 978-3-425-14098-8

You know Ruby, don't you? Ruby the parrot? She lives with a boy called Rajiv, in London. Ruby, Rajiv and his family live in Notting Hill – that's in the west of London.

But that's not where Ruby is from. Ruby is from a country called Guyana. That's far away, in South America.

ENGLAND

London

NORTH ATLANTIC OCEAN

GUYANA

SOUTH AMERICA

N
NW NE
W E
SW SE
S

In Guyana, Ruby lived with her family in the rainforest.
She lived with her mum, her dad and her two brothers.
They lived there in the trees, near a river.

Every day Ruby and her brothers played together in the
trees. And every day their dad told them, "Don't fly too
far away. Don't fly over the ocean. The North Atlantic
Ocean is a dangerous place!"

Ruby and her brothers listened to their dad, but they
still tried to fly high enough to see the North Atlantic

Ocean. Was it really that dangerous?! They flew through the trees, looking for fruit. Her brothers loved pineapples, but Ruby always looked for bananas. Oh, how she loved them!

One afternoon, Ruby and her brothers were flying around the treetops. Suddenly it got very dark. There were big, black clouds everywhere. It started to rain. And it was windy. Really windy! What a storm!

Ruby tried to fly in the storm but it was too difficult. Finally she decided to find a tree to sit in. She looked for her brothers but couldn't see them. It was too dark.

Ruby was a bit scared. She was also tired from flying in the storm. After a while she fell asleep. She had a wonderful dream ... It was her birthday, and her present was a giant banana! The banana was bigger than she was, and there were nine candles in it — Ruby would be nine on her next birthday.

When she woke up it was morning. The storm was over and the sky was blue. Lots of birds and other parrots were flying through the trees. She called out to her brothers. Nothing. Where were they?! She looked around. There were trees everywhere, but they weren't *her* trees. Ruby was lost.

She flew up, high above the trees. She flew up high into the sky. She could see everything below her now. So many trees, so many birds and parrots. But she couldn't see her family. Poor Ruby was scared. And hungry.

She decided to look for something to eat. Food first, family later! Ruby flew for a while. Maybe she would find a giant banana, like in her dream! Ruby started thinking about that giant banana again … how yummy it had looked ... and all for her, for her birthday …

Ten minutes later, she finally looked down again and saw ... the sea! Well, the ocean actually. Ruby remembered what her dad always said – "The North Atlantic Ocean is a dangerous place." The North Atlantic Ocean ... and what a huge ocean it was! Ruby looked down and saw boats everywhere! She was excited! It didn't look dangerous …

Below her, Ruby saw a big yellow boat. It looked a bit like the banana from her dream. Her tummy made a noise. She was still hungry!

Ruby flew over the boat. "What is that smell?!" she
wondered. It smelt like … bananas! She saw lots of
big, big boxes on the boat. She flew closer and – yes!
– they were boxes of bananas! There were lots and lots
and LOTS of boxes … and they were full of bananas!
They smelt so good. "Is this a dream?!" she wondered.

Ruby flew lower and landed on the boat. One little box was open. "Can I take a banana?!" she asked herself. "I'll have just one …" she decided.

Well, that banana was so good, and Ruby was so hungry, that she decided to have just one more. And maybe one more. Suddenly, Ruby was tired and sleepy … she fell asleep right there on her banana bed in the banana box!

When Ruby woke up it was dark. She missed her family. How would she find them now? The banana boat was in the middle of the North Atlantic Ocean. She was so far away from home. She wanted to fly back to them but she didn't know which way to go! "Maybe Dad is right and the Ocean is dangerous," she thought. She decided to stay on the boat – it was safe and full of bananas!

So Ruby stayed on that boat for six days. She ate lots of bananas. Every night she slept on her banana bed and every morning she flew above the boat. All she could see was the ocean! Just water, everywhere. But one morning she saw something different. She saw land! "What country is that?!" Ruby wondered.

The next day Ruby woke up, had a banana and then flew above the boat to look for land again ... but she didn't see just land, she saw buildings and people, too! They were in a port. It was raining. Ruby didn't know where she was. "What country is this? What city?" she thought. Then she heard a man say in a loud voice, "Welcome to Portsmouth. How was your trip? Sorry about the rain – I'm sure the weather in South America was much nicer than here in England!"

So she was in England, then. In Portsmouth. People were taking the bananas off the boat now. The boxes of bananas were big and heavy. But not Ruby's box — there was only one banana left in *her* box! She decided it was time for her to leave, too.

So, with the last banana in her claws, she flew up high into the sky and left that yellow banana boat behind. She looked down. Portsmouth looked very different to Guyana. No rainforests. Just lots of buildings and lots of streets. So many cars, buses, boats and trains. There was a train right below Ruby. The sun suddenly came out from behind a cloud and it stopped raining. Ruby flew in circles above the train. It was so good to fly over land again!

Ruby flew above the train for about an hour. It was fun, watching the little people getting onto and off the train. At every station Ruby flew down and listened to the people. What a funny kind of English! It wasn't like the English they spoke in Guyana. She liked listening to it.

Finally, the train came into a big station. Ruby flew down and landed on the top of the train. It was banana time!

She ate her banana and looked around. "London Waterloo", the sign on the platform said. London. Ruby knew about London. "The Queen lives in London. I'd like to see the Queen!" she thought.

So she flew up above the station again and looked around. She couldn't see the Queen but she could see a big river. This river was a bit different to her river at home, but she liked it.

Ruby flew lower. She flew past lots of buildings along the river. She flew past one big silver building and saw another parrot! She slowed down and flew towards the silver building. The other parrot was flying towards her. She was so excited! She waved her wing and it waved back. She called out, "Hello! Fly with me!" and the parrot did. It started to fly next to her ... but when she looked around a few seconds later, the parrot was gone. It was just her reflection.

Ruby was suddenly very lonely. She missed her family. She was so far away from home. She wanted to fly through the trees with her brothers again.

Ruby flew up to a bridge and sat on top of it. "I need to find some trees," she decided. "That will make me feel better." So she looked around and there, on the other side of the river, she saw some trees.

Ruby flew across the river. Soon she was flying over the trees. It was a big park. There were lots of families sitting on the grass and having a picnic.

She looked for a nice tree to sit in. She found one quickly – but she couldn't find any bananas. She found a nut in the tree and ate that – but it was hard and small and it just wasn't as good as a banana!

She looked down. Not far from her tree there was a family having a picnic. There was a boy, his parents and his grandma. The boy was playing a guitar. His mum was reading a book and his dad was ... wait a minute ... his dad was eating a banana! Oh, it looked so good and it was so close! Ruby's tummy made a noise.

And do you know what cheeky Ruby did next? She flew down from the tree and took that banana! The boy's dad was quite shocked! "Look at that parrot!" he said. "It took my banana!" The boy looked at his dad, and then at Ruby, and started to laugh. "It's not funny, Rajiv!" said Rajiv's dad. "That was *my* banana!"

Rajiv went to the tree and looked up at Ruby. "She must be hungry," he said. He went to the picnic basket. "Here, Dad, have another one." He gave his dad another banana – and he gave another one to Ruby, too! He winked at her, sat down and started to play his guitar again.

Well, Ruby was so happy. She flew down with her
banana and sat next to Rajiv. He was her new best
friend. Rajiv thought Ruby was pretty cool, too. In fact,
when the picnic was over, he wanted to take Ruby home
with him. Ruby liked this idea but Rajiv's dad didn't.
"You can't have a pet parrot, Rajiv," he said. "Just no."

But Ruby followed them home. She flew above them all
the way back to Notting Hill. Rajiv's dad closed the front
door and told her to go away, but she didn't. She sat
outside their front door all night.

In the morning, she flew up and looked through Rajiv's window. She tapped her beak on the glass. Tap, tap, tap! Rajiv woke up. He opened the window and Ruby flew in. She sat on his bed, looking at him. "Bananas!" she squawked, "Bananas!" Rajiv laughed, and said, "Wow, you really love bananas, don't you?!"

Quietly, Rajiv got a banana from the kitchen. Ten minutes later his mum came in to wake him up. She looked at Ruby, opened her mouth to say something ... and then just shook her head and said, "I'll tell your dad you've got a pet – but YOU have to look after her!"

And he did. That was three years ago now, and Ruby
still lives with Rajiv. He gives her a banana every day.
Sometimes she still misses her family in Guyana, but
she's got a new family now. She loves all of Rajiv's
family and friends. His dad even likes her now, too.

When Ruby goes to sleep at night in Rajiv's room, she thinks how lucky she is to be with him – and for her next birthday, she and Rajiv will go back to Hyde Park, where that first picnic was, so she can play with all the birds who live there. Ruby can't wait for that.

Vokabelliste

Seite 3	country	Land
	South America	Südamerika

Seite 4	rainforest	Regenwald
	ocean	Ozean, Meer

Seite 5	treetop	Baumwipfel

Seite 6	she fell asleep	sie schlief ein
	giant	riesig

Seite 7	when she woke up	als sie aufwachte
	actually	eigentlich
	huge	riesig

Seite 8	smell	Geruch

Seite 9	lower	tiefer

Seite 10	she missed	sie vermisste

Seite 11	building	Gebäude
	port	Hafen

Seite 12	heavy	schwer
	claw	Kralle
	she left behind	sie ließ zurück

Seite 14	they spoke	sie sprachen
	on the top of	(oben) auf
	sign	Schild
	platform	Bahnsteig
Seite 15	past	vorbei an
	she slowed down	sie wurde langsamer
	towards	in Richtung
	a few seconds	ein paar Sekunden
Seite 16	lonely	einsam
	across	über
Seite 17	nut	Nuss
	close	nah
Seite 18	cheeky	frech
	he winked at her	er zwinkerte ihr zu
Seite 19	in fact	genau genommen
	front door	Haustür
Seite 20	she tapped	sie klopfte
	beak	Schnabel
	she squawked	sie kreischte
	she shook	sie schüttelte
Seite 22	go to sleep	schlafen gehen